This Annual belongs to

Age

Favourite player

Prediction of the Rams' final position this season

Prediction of Sky Bet Championship winners this season

Prediction of FA Cup winners this season

Prediction of EFL Cup winners this season

Prediction of teams to be promoted
to the Premier League this season:

1st

2nd

Play-Off winners

Written by twocan
Contributors: Rob Mason, Peter Rogers

A TWOCAN PUBLICATION

©2016. Published by twocan under licence
from Derby County Football Club.

ISBN 978-1-909872-82-0

C000178690

CONTENTS

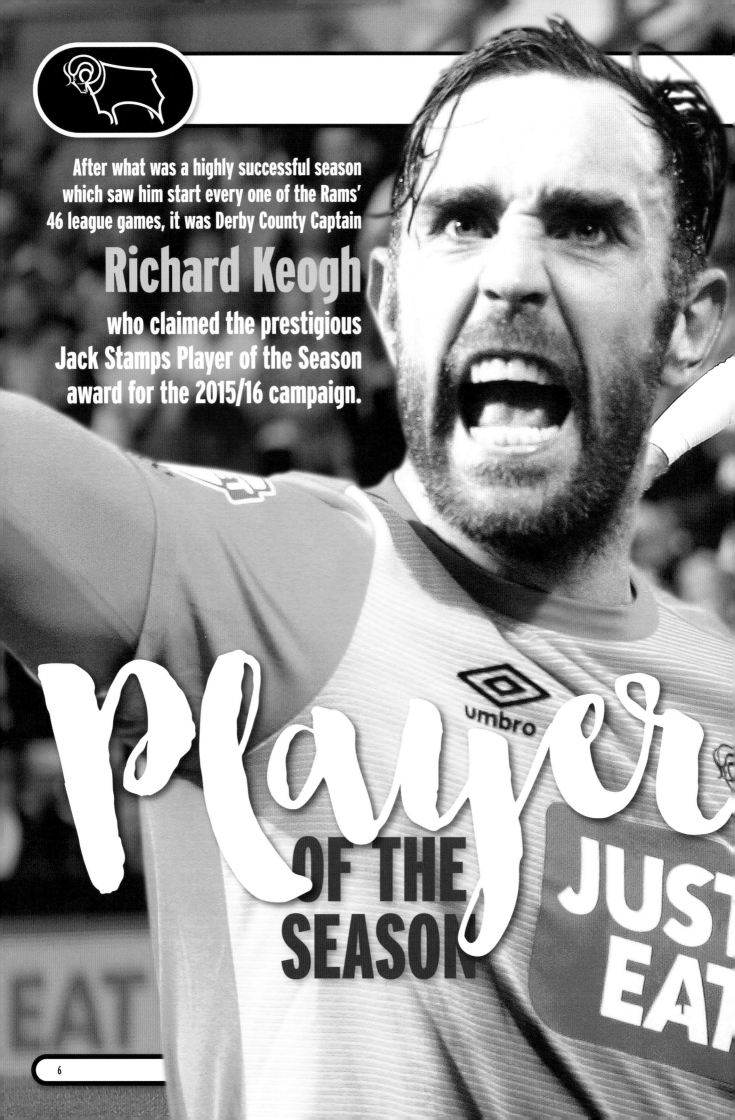

After what was a highly successful season which saw him start every one of the Rams' 46 league games, it was Derby County Captain **Richard Keogh** who claimed the prestigious Jack Stamps Player of the Season award for the 2015/16 campaign.

Player

OF THE

SEASON

As well as winning the Player of the Season award, it was a clean sweep for Keogh as he also picked up the Players' Player of the Season and the Supporters Club Player of the Season awards.

In a season of mixed emotions for the Rams, narrowly missing out on a promotion, it was certainly an eventful one to remember for Keogh, as it saw him regain his captaincy in the latter stages of the season.

The chants of his name could be heard during the season as he was a model of consistency in the team and the fans commended him for his bravery and commitment on the pitch.

A stand out game in particular for the Republic of Ireland international came early on in the season in front of a home crowd when Derby beat Rotherham emphatically 3-0 - with Keogh scoring the third and final goal.

However, it was his collective performances that earned him plaudits from the fans, the coaching staff and also the media as he helped inspire 20 clean sheets for the team and concede just 46 goals throughout the course of the season.

After the season concluded, the action did not stop for Keogh as he was straight on the plane for the UEFA European Championships in France and as he featured in arguably Ireland's most crucial two games of the season.

Keogh broke into the side against Italy in what was the final group game of the competition and helped inspire a shock 1-0 victory to progress into the knockout stages.

Although he was unable to deny the hosts France from progressing past Ireland in the round of 16, it was something of a dream for Keogh to be playing a crucial part for his nation in a major competition and it was an experience which seemed a fitting way to end what was a spectacular season for the Derby County Captain.

THE Squad 2016-17

Cyrus CHRISTIE | 02

POSITION: Defender   NATIONALITY: Irish   DOB: 30.09.1992

DID YOU KNOW? Cyrus was named the Sammy Crooks Young Player of the Year for 2015/16 and he was also part of the Republic of Ireland's Euro 2016 squad.

Scott CARSON | 01

POSITION: Goalkeeper   NATIONALITY: English   DOB: 03.09.1985

DID YOU KNOW? Scott played 39 times in all competitions last season and kept 16 clean sheets, helping the Rams reach the play-offs.

Craig FORSYTH | 03

POSITION: Defender   NATIONALITY: Scottish   DOB: 24.02.1989

DID YOU KNOW? Scotland international left-back Craig, is set to miss the rest of the 2016/17 season after suffering a long-term knee injury in August.

Craig BRYSON | 04

POSITION: Midfielder   **NATIONALITY:** Scottish   **DOB:** 06.11.1986

DID YOU KNOW? After recovering from a knee injury in last season's opening fixture, Craig came back to play a key part for the squad's push for promotion.

Jason SHACKELL | 05

POSITION: Defender   **NATIONALITY:** English   **DOB:** 27.09.1983

DID YOU KNOW? In his first season back at the club, Jason started in all 46 of the club's 2015/16 games. He also hit the back of the net twice in all competitions.

THE Squad 2016-17

Richard KEOGH | 06

POSITION: Defender   NATIONALITY: Irish   DOB: 11.08.1986

DID YOU KNOW? Richard won a clean sweep of the club's Player of the Year awards in May 2016 and went on to represent the Republic of Ireland at Euro 2016 in France.

Johnny RUSSELL | 07

POSITION: Striker   NATIONALITY: Scottish   DOB: 08.04.1990

DID YOU KNOW? Scottish international Johnny made 50 appearances for the Rams last season and hit double figures in front of goal with ten strikes.

Ikechi
ANYA | 08

POSITION: Midfielder   NATIONALITY: Scottish   DOB: 03.01.1988

DID YOU KNOW? Scotland international Anya, who is predominately a winger but can also play at full-back, signed on transfer deadline Day from Premier League side Watford.

Tom
INCE | 10

POSITION: Midfielder   NATIONALITY: English   DOB: 30.01.1992

DID YOU KNOW? Tom, who has represented England at U17, U19 and U21 level, scored his first professional hat-trick in the 4-0 thrashing of Bristol City in late 2015.

Darren
BENT | 11

POSITION: Striker   NATIONALITY: English   DOB: 06.02.1984

DID YOU KNOW? Darren, who has 13 full England caps and four international goals to his name, netted some crucial goals last season as the Rams pushed for the Premier League.

THE squad 2016-17

James WILSON | 14

POSITION: Striker   NATIONALITY: English   DOB: 01.12.1995

DID YOU KNOW? A graduate of Manchester Utd's famed Academy, England U21 striker James made the season-long switch from the Red Devils to the Rams in the summer.

Chris BAIRD | 12

POSITION: Defender   NATIONALITY: Northern Irish   DOB: 25.02.1982

DID YOU KNOW? Versatile Chris, helped Northern Ireland reach the Euro 2016 Finals and started his county's tournament opener against Poland.

Bradley JOHNSON | 15

POSITION: Midfielder   NATIONALITY: English   DOB: 28.04.1987

DID YOU KNOW? Bradley played 33 times for the Rams last season and won the club's Goal of the Season award for his strike in the 4-0 home thumping of Hull City.

Alex PEARCE | 16

POSITION: Defender   **NATIONALITY:** Irish   **DOB:** 09.11.1988

DID YOU KNOW? Alex scored on his debut for the Republic of Ireland in a 4-1 victory over Oman in 2012. Ironically, his second goal came against the same opposition in 2014.

Jacob BUTTERFIELD | 18

POSITION: Midfielder   **NATIONALITY:** English   **DOB:** 10.06.1990

DID YOU KNOW? In Jacob's impressive first season with the Rams, he pulled on the Derby shirt 40 times and found the back of the net on eight occasions.

Will
HUGHES | 19

POSITION: Midfielder   NATIONALITY: English   DOB: 07.04.1995

DID YOU KNOW? A product of the Derby County Academy, Will's attack-minded midfield displays and growing list of Man of the Match awards make him a fans' favourite.

Abdoul
CAMARA | 20

POSITION: Midfielder   NATIONALITY: Guinean   DOB: 20.02.1990

DID YOU KNOW? Guinea international Abdoul, made the move to the iPro Stadium from French top-flight side Angers SCO during the 2016 January transfer window.

THE
Squad
2016-17

Matej VYDRA | 23

POSITION: Striker   NATIONALITY: Czech   DOB: 01.05.1992

DID YOU KNOW? Czech Republic international striker Matej, arrived at the iPro Stadium from Premier League side Watford towards the end of August 2016.

Nick BLACKMAN | 22

POSITION: Striker   NATIONALITY: English   DOB: 11.11.1989

DID YOU KNOW? Nick joined Derby from fellow Sky Bet Championship side Reading in January 2016 and made 17 appearances during the second half of the campaign.

Andreas WEIMANN | 24

POSITION: Striker   NATIONALITY: Austrian   DOB: 05.08.1991

DID YOU KNOW? Austrian international Andreas joined the Rams from Aston Villa at the beginning of last season and went on to play 33 games and grab four goals.

Max
LOWE | 25

POSITION: Defender   NATIONALITY: English   DOB: 11.05.1997

DID YOU KNOW? Comfortable at left-back or midfield, England youth international Max made his senior debut in August 2016 in the EFL cup.

Marcus
OLSSON | 29

POSITION: Defender   NATIONALITY: Swedish   DOB: 17.05.1988

DID YOU KNOW? Signed in January 2016, Marcus became a big hit with the fans after netting his first goal in the 1-0 home win over arch-rivals Nottingham Forest in March.

Jamie
HANSON | 26

POSITION: Defender/Midfielder   NATIONALITY: English   DOB: 10.11.1995

DID YOU KNOW? Another product of Derby County's Academy, Jamie made first-team bow in 2015, scoring a debut goal direct from a corner in a 1-1 draw at Norwich City.

Timi
ELSNIK | 30

POSITION: Midfielder   NATIONALITY: Slovenian   DOB: 29.04.1998

DID YOU KNOW? Slovenian attacking midfielder Timi had a great 2015/16! He won the Scholar of the Year award and also part of the U21's promotion-winning squad.

Farrend RAWSON | 31

POSITION: Defender   NATIONALITY: English   DOB: 11.07.1996

DID YOU KNOW? A commanding centre-half with a strong and powerful presence, Farrend spent the 2015/16 campaign on loan to fellow Championship side Rotherham Utd.

George THORNE | 34

POSITION: Midfielder   NATIONALITY: English   DOB: 04.01.1993

DID YOU KNOW? After playing in 36 games and scoring one of the Goal of the Season contenders, George's campaign ended with a broken leg in the final fixture of 2015/16.

Chris WEALE | 32

POSITION: Goalkeeper   NATIONALITY: English   DOB: 09.02.1982

DID YOU KNOW? Chris signed at the end of August 2016 and brings with him a wealth of experience, having made 415 appearances in English football before joining the Rams.

Jonathan MITCHELL | 35

POSITION: Goalkeeper   NATIONALITY: English   DOB: 24.11.1994

DID YOU KNOW? Jonathan made his professional debut for Derby in a 2-1 FA Cup Third Round victory over his hometown club Hartlepool United in January 2016.

JOHNNY
Russell

7

A 12-match unbeaten run in the League at the beginning of the season included Roy McFarland scoring in the 1-1 draw with Chelsea

Alan Hinton finished top of the scoring chart with 15 goals

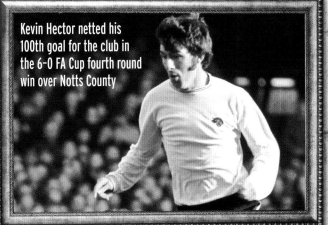

Kevin Hector netted his 100th goal for the club in the 6-0 FA Cup fourth round win over Notts County

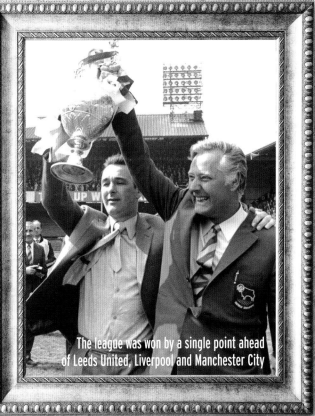

The league was won by a single point ahead of Leeds United, Liverpool and Manchester City

Record signing Colin Todd was voted the club's Player of the Season

spot the Season

Can you spot the season from these five clues?

Fan'TASTIC!

Can you find them all?

ANSWERS ON PAGE 62

SKILLS: THE RAINBOW KICK

1 Start off with your feet on either side of the ball

2 Use one foot to roll the ball up your other leg

3 Make sure to roll the ball hard enough to give it some air

4 When the ball is in the air strike it with your heel

5 ...and flick it over your head!

Brazilian star striker, Neymar, is well known for his use of the rainbow kick on the pitch and regularly fools his opposition. The trick is an impressive show of skill which takes practise, practise practise!

TIP: Lean forward as you're doing the trick, this helps create space between you and the ball so you can strike it more easily.

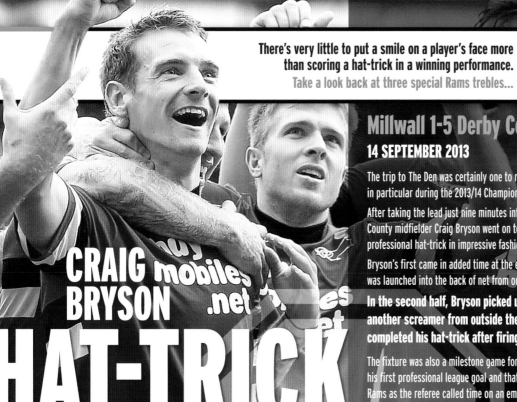

There's very little to put a smile on a player's face more than scoring a hat-trick in a winning performance. Take a look back at three special Rams trebles...

CRAIG BRYSON HAT-TRICK

Millwall 1-5 Derby County

14 SEPTEMBER 2013

The trip to The Den was certainly one to remember for fans and one Derby player in particular during the 2013/14 Championship season.

After taking the lead just nine minutes into the game courtesy of Jake Buxton, Derby County midfielder Craig Bryson went on to thrive in the contest - netting his first professional hat-trick in impressive fashion.

Bryson's first came in added time at the end of the opening half after a neatly struck ball was launched into the back of net from outside the box.

In the second half, Bryson picked up where he left off, converting another screamer from outside the box and with nine minutes remaining, completed his hat-trick after firing home a lay-off from Kieron Freeman.

The fixture was also a milestone game for young starlet Mason Bennett as he netted his first professional league goal and that proved to be the icing on the cake for the Rams as the referee called time on an emphatic 5-1 victory away from home.

Derby County 5-0 Nottingham Forest

22 MARCH 2014

For Derby fans everywhere, this was a day for sure that will go down in history as the Rams achieved a record-equalling victory over their local rivals from across the A52.

5-0 was the scoreline and it was a day of record-breaking, as not only was it the biggest Derby victory over Nottingham Forest for 116 years, but it was also the first time since Steve Bloomer in 1898 that a Derby player had recorded a hat-trick in such a crucial game.

Having scored his first professional hat-trick just six months earlier, Craig Bryson continued his fine form in front of goal and netted six minutes into the game after the lively midfielder burst into the box to smash the ball home. Just after the half-an-hour mark, Derby were two goals in front of their rivals and Bryson had two goals to his name after a fine lay-off from Chris Martin inside the box allowed the Scottish international the space to direct the ball into the bottom left corner of the goal.

Two further goals were scored by Derby, courtesy of Jeff Hendrick and Johnny Russell, before a penalty was awarded in the 69th minute and it was Bryson who stepped up to write himself into the history books and draw the curtain on what was a remarkable day for the Rams.

CRAIG BRYSON HEROES

TOM INCE

Derby County 4-0 Bristol City

15 DECEMBER 2015

In what was a cold winter evening in late December at the iPro Stadium, Tom Ince rewarded the Derby fans with a greatly received early Christmas present - netting his first hat-trick in professional football after scoring twice on several occasions previously.

After knocking on the door during the early stages of the game, Ince's first goal came three minutes before the half-time interval after a good individual break allowed him the space to break into the box and slot the ball past former Rams 'keeper Frank Fielding.

Eager to further his goal tally, Ince continued his impressive display and netted again from close range to double Derby's lead and with the hat-trick very much on, he scored just eight minutes later after a generous pass from Darren Bent to claim the match ball.

All round, it was a great night for the Rams and Johnny Russell wrapped up the game five minutes after Ince's hat trick, heading the ball into the top corner of the net from an impressive cross by Chris Baird in a fine 4-0 win.

IKECHI *Anya*

8

WILL HUGHES

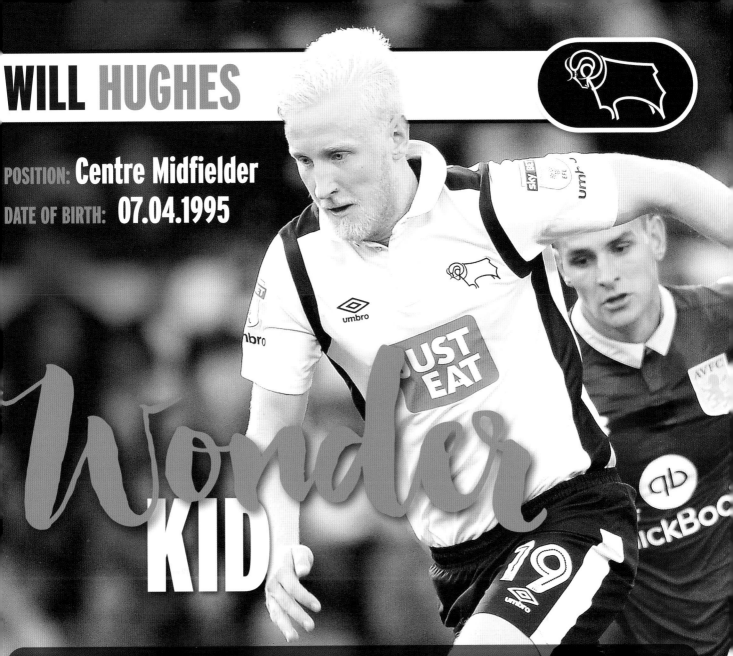

POSITION: Centre Midfielder
DATE OF BIRTH: 07.04.1995

Wonder **KID**

Hughes is a graduate of Repton School and has gone from strength-to-strength since arriving from Nottingham Forest as a 12-year-old, which resulted in him signing professional terms in the spring of 2012.

Hughes has bags of ability and, as you would expect as a midfielder, he can see a pass and he can unlock opposition defences. His outstanding displays have earned plenty of plaudits in recent years and he has established himself as a key player at the iPro Stadium.

After impressing in Derby's Under-18s as a first-year scholar in the early months of the 2011/12 season he was handed his first-team debut as a 16-year-old by coming off the bench in Derby's 3-2 loss at Peterborough United in November 2011.

He was called up by England at Under-17 level in March 2012 and found the net in the Algarve Tournament against Holland, before returning to make an impact at first-team level before the season was out.

He made his first-ever start for the club on the final day of the season in the home game against Peterborough, where he produced an eye-catching display on the right-hand side of midfield.

2012/13 saw Hughes rack up 38 appearances, scoring twice, and earn his first England U21 caps. His form attracted interest from afar but he remained focused on his performances for Derby, and he further blossomed in the 2013/14 season.

He made 48 appearances in total and scored five goals, including a fine back-heeled finish in the Play-Off Semi-Final win over Brighton & Hove Albion at the iPro Stadium, and was also named in the PFA Championship Team of the Season.

In 2014/15 his performance level was cranked up a notch and he appeared 48 times in all competitions, with his form going on to earn him the Player of the Year, Jack Stamps Player of the Year and Supporters' Club Player of the Year Awards.

Despite having a strong start to pre-season, Hughes endured a hugely frustrating beginning to the 2015/16 season as he suffered a serious knee injury on the opening fixture of the campaign against Bolton Wanderers.

He returned to first team action in April 2016 against, ironically, Bolton and played a starring role from there on, producing a string of Man of the Match displays along the way.

A
Newcastle were relegated to the Championship last season after finishing 18th, but this club was bottom of the table

B
The creatures present on Brentford's club crest

C
Spanish midfielder who joined the Canaries from Liverpool in the summer

D
Preston North End play their home games here

E
Wolves midfielder who was in Wales' squad for Euro 2016

F
Name of Brighton's stadium before it was sponsored by AMEX

G
Reading's top appearance maker last season

26

H
Blackburn's player of the 2015/16 season

I
Scored twelve goals for the Rams from midfield last season

Leeds United's kit manufacturer

J
Wigan's Finnish goalie who helped them reach promotion last season

K

L
Huddersfield played their home games here before the John Smith's Stadium

M
The scorer of Birmingham's winning goal when they won the League Cup in 2011

Quite often, they might have to play two matches within three or four days of each other and over the course of a season, regular players could play in the region of 50 games!

That would be a lot if they were simply running as a long distance runner does. In football though, that running is done with a mixture of short sprints from a standing start and runs of various lengths at differing intensities. On top of this, there is a lot of twisting and turning, often while someone is trying to pull the player back or even kick them.

If they can cope with this, there is then the consideration that once the footballer has the ball, they have to use it, either with a telling pass or a shot on goal, while the opposition do all they can to stop them. Added to this is the fact that the thousands of fans watching in the stadium and the millions viewing on TV are only too ready to criticise them if they do not get it right.

FOOTY Fitness

To cope with all this, players have to be supremely fit so they have the stamina to last 90 minutes on a regular basis, and have the competitive edge to deal with opponents trying to stop them. Players also have to be careful to eat and drink the right things, get the right amount of sleep and keep themselves in tip-top shape.

In the summer when players return from a few weeks off, they do a lot of physical training to get themselves ready for the big kick-off. Once a few games have been played and they have, what players call, 'match-fitness', their aim is to maintain that fitness, but not over-do things.

Most players will train for two or three hours most days and do additional work in the gym, as well as perhaps doing pilates or yoga to help look after their bodies. Cycling and swimming can be useful too, but so is knowing when to simply rest, because the Championship season is a long and gruelling campaign.

18

JACOB

Butterfield

On the Road

Do you know where every Championship team plays their home games?
Fill in the missing words and find all the grounds in the grid!

S	R	F	C	A	R	R	O	W	R	O	A	D	S	L	N	A	L	F	S	J	D
E	A	T	O	A	K	W	E	L	L	S	T	A	D	I	U	M	U	K	V	O	F
Y	S	K	W	S	R	I	A	E	K	O	W	O	N	T	F	E	X	B	A	H	G
Q	I	F	M	V	M	D	R	S	J	G	L	D	S	A	W	X	C	T	X	N	I
W	S	K	U	I	U	L	I	B	H	E	S	N	J	O	M	S	I	S	D	S	P
N	K	G	I	L	I	E	C	F	S	T	B	H	O	U	C	T	T	M	A	M	M
A	E	R	D	L	D	M	V	Y	F	A	O	D	G	Y	L	A	Y	U	O	I	U
P	L	I	A	A	A	R	G	L	D	C	P	N	Y	E	N	D	G	I	R	T	I
O	A	F	T	P	T	U	J	R	O	A	I	S	G	D	Y	I	R	D	D	H	D
R	D	F	S	A	S	V	D	V	R	F	J	T	R	A	H	U	O	A	N	S	A
T	P	I	W	R	I	E	C	K	O	B	T	E	Y	C	T	M	U	T	A	S	T
M	E	N	D	K	K	Z	M	T	M	D	W	U	G	S	K	E	N	S	L	T	S
A	E	P	L	D	S	B	P	A	S	S	O	T	S	F	T	B	D	O	L	A	I
N	D	A	R	Q	J	F	H	N	J	I	M	Y	Z	R	U	A	O	R	E	D	L
R	C	R	A	V	E	N	C	O	T	T	A	G	E	D	O	E	D	P	N	I	L
O	U	K	E	H	D	P	V	J	F	M	S	P	C	I	P	A	R	I	G	U	E
A	E	S	S	E	A	L	N	E	W	Y	O	R	K	S	T	A	D	I	U	M	R
D	N	W	X	A	M	U	I	D	A	T	S	X	U	E	N	I	L	O	M	M	I
H	I	L	L	S	B	O	R	O	U	G	H	Q	O	H	G	S	G	E	A	T	P

Aston Villa	_____ Park	**Cardiff**	_____ City Stadium	**Nottm Forest**	City _____
Barnsley	_____ Stadium	**Derby**	_____ Stadium	**Preston**	_____
Birmingham	St _____	**Fulham**	Craven _____	**QPR**	_____ Road
Blackburn	_____ Park	**Huddersfield**	John_____ Stadium	**Reading**	_____ Stadium
Brentford	Griffin ____	**Ipswich**	_____ Road	**Rotherham**	AESSEAL ___ Stadium
Brighton	_____ Stadium	**Leeds**	Elland ____	**Sheff Wed**	_____
Bristol City	_____ Gate	**Newcastle**	St _____ Park	**Wigan**	DW _____
Burton	_____ Stadium	**Norwich**	_____ Road	**Wolves**	_____ Stadium

CHAMPIONSHIP DANGER MEN

ASTON VILLA
ROSS McCORMACK

One of the costliest strikers in the Championship, Scotland international McCormack cost Fulham £11m in 2014 with the Cottagers making a profit of £1m when Villa bought the Glasgow born hot-shot at the start of this season. The 30-year-old has scored over 150 goals in his career and is a man who makes many more.

BARNSLEY
TOM BRADSHAW

Having scored 20 goals in each of the last two seasons, Bradshaw was disappointed to lose to Barnsley in last season's League One Play-offs for Walsall - but then signed for the Tykes. Having scored a League Cup hat-trick against Championship side Forest last season, the Wales international got his first goal in this season's Championship in a South Yorkshire derby against Rotherham at the end of August.

BIRMINGHAM CITY
CLAYTON DONALDSON

Jamaican international Donaldson is a great spearhead for Blues. Good in the air, determined and mobile, he has scored over 40 goals for three different clubs and could equal that achievement with a good season for Birmingham, for whom he has bagged 27 in the past two seasons.

BLACKBURN ROVERS
DANNY GRAHAM

A well-travelled target man, Danny Graham impressed on loan for Rovers last season before signing for them in the summer. With well over 100 goals in his career, Graham's best haul was 27 with Watford in 2010/11 - 24 of those were in the Championship in what was his last full season spent at this level.

BRENTFORD
SCOTT HOGAN

Hogan could be a hero for the Bees this season and be their secret weapon. Having played for six non-league clubs, he was given a chance by Rochdale who he had played for at Academy level. Hogan quickly made up for lost time, a debut goal being Sky TV's 'Goal of the Day'. It was the first of 19 he got that season as he fired Rochdale to promotion, was voted Player of the Year and into the PFA League 2 team. Badly injured soon after a move to Brentford, he returned with seven goals in seven games late last season.

BRIGHTON & HOVE ALBION
TOMER HEMED

The 29-year-old Israel international is a big part of Brighton's promotion hopes. Having played in Spain as well as his home country, Hemed scored 16 goals in 40 games in his first season in English football last term and Chris Hughton will look to bring the best out of him once again this time round.

Watch out for these dangermen when the Rams meet their Championship rivals...

BRISTOL CITY
TAMMY ABRAHAM

With 74 goals in 98 games for Chelsea at youth level, the question is, can England U20 speed merchant Abraham do it at first team level? Given a Chelsea debut v Liverpool last season, it took 15 minutes of his debut on loan to Bristol City to find the net and did so four more times in his next five games. If Tammy keeps it up he could be this season's 'Rockin' Robin'.

BURTON ALBION
CHRIS O'GRADY

O'Grady has had so many loans he might think he's a high street bank, his current stint with Burton being his tenth. On loan from Brighton, Chris started this season three goals short of a century. Not always prolific, he can be - netting 15 in 2013/14 - but he is always a handful and is key to Burton doing well this season following last year's promotion.

CARDIFF CITY
RICKIE LAMBERT

Approaching 250 career goals - over 100 of them for one club (Southampton) - Rickie Lambert is a lethal finisher. The sheer number of his goals earned him an England debut in 2013 and he scored with his first touch, heading home against Scotland. Now 32, Lambert isn't the quickest, but his game has never been based on pace.

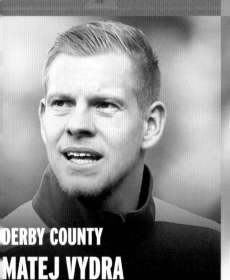

DERBY COUNTY
MATEJ VYDRA

The Rams paid a reported £8m to snap up the 24-year-old Czech Republic hitman who was the Championship Player of the Year in 2013 after netting 20 goals in 41 games for Watford. A nippy goal-poacher Vydra played in his home country as well as Italy and Belgium before coming into English football where he has also played for WBA and Reading.

FULHAM
SONE ALUKO

Nigerian international Sone Aluko joined Fulham from Hull City in the summer, having enjoyed two promotions with the Tigers and picking up an FA Cup runners-up medal in 2014. He is an intelligent player with quick feet and has the confidence in his own ability to fill gap left behind by Ross McCormack's and Moussa Dembele's departures.

HUDDERSFIELD TOWN
NAHKI WELLS

Having hit 17 goals last season, Wells will hope to maintain that level of consistency for the Terriers. Nahki came to the fore at nearby Bradford City for whom he played in the League Cup final in 2013 after scoring in the semi-final against Aston Villa. Pacey, persistent and with the ability to finish, Wells is always a tough customer.

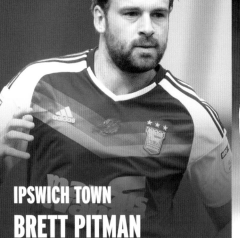

IPSWICH TOWN
BRETT PITMAN

A consistent goal-scorer who notched 11 goals for the Tractor Boys last season and 14 the year before as part of Bournemouth's title-winning team. Following Ipswich's sale of Daryl Murphy to Newcastle at the start of the season, the club's need for Pitman to be among the goals will be even more important this time round.

LEEDS UNITED
CHRIS WOOD

Twice a promotion winner to the Premier League, Leeds will hope Wood can complete a notable hat-trick at Elland Road. A New Zealand international who played at the World Cup finals in 2010, Chris won promotion to the Championship with Brighton and into the top flight with both West Brom and Leicester.

NEWCASTLE UNITED
DWIGHT GAYLE

Lift off for the man whose first club was Stansted came when Newcastle United paid £10m to bring the Londoner from Crystal Palace. Gayle's first ever Premier League goal came against Newcastle in his Palace days and he made a good start at firing the Magpies back towards the top flight with four goals in his first four games for Rafa Benitez's side.

NORWICH CITY
SERGI CANOS

A former Barcelona youth player, Sergi played once for Liverpool before spending last season on loan to Brentford where he scored seven and made five goals as a winger. Still a teenager, the Spain U19 international cost the Canaries £2.5m in the summer to bring him from Anfield and he could well be a potent weapon whenever he is on the ball for City.

NOTTINGHAM FOREST
BRITT ASSOMBALONGA

23 goals in 43 games for Peterborough in 2013/14 signalled Assombalonga's goal threat, Posh having already recognised that when making the Watford Academy product their record signing. A bad injury cost Britt 14 months of his career having also broken Forest's transfer record but with 19 goals in his first 36 games he remains one of the hottest properties in the Championship.

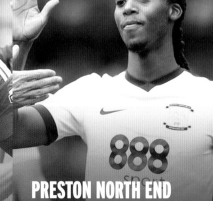

PRESTON NORTH END
DANIEL JOHNSON

Given a new contract early this season, Johnson is Preston's midfield creator and offers a goal threat coming in from the left. Having been schooled in the youth systems at Palace and Villa, the Jamaican came to Preston in January 2015, helped North End to promotion and is at the heart of much of their best attacking play.

QUEENS PARK RANGERS
TJARONN CHERY

Hoops' Player of the Year last season, Tjaronn scored three goals in the first four games of this season, his first campaign in English football. Now 28, Chery was called into an international squad for Holland in May 2015 after scoring 15 times in his last season with Gronigen.

READING
YANN KERMORGANT

The aerial ability of the veteran French striker can be a key asset for Jaap Stam's side. Kermorgant helped Bournemouth to the Championship title in 2015 when he scored 17 goals in all competitions and was nominated for the Championship goal of the season for one of his trademark bicycle kicks.

ROTHERHAM UNITED
DANNY WARD

Rotherham will fight hard to stay up this year with Danny Ward a key man for the Millers. He scored on the opening day of the season against Wolves and soon followed that up with a vital winner against Brentford. On his day he can be lethal, as he showed with a Championship hat-trick away to Watford in May 2014 in his Huddersfield days. 25 just before Christmas, Ward's form is likely to be key to Rotherham's progress.

SHEFFIELD WEDNESDAY
STEVEN FLETCHER

Scotland international striker Fletcher spent the latter part of last season in France with Marseille - making his debut against PSG when he came on for Michy Batshuayi who Chelsea have since paid mega-money for. One of the best headers of the ball in the game, the former Hibs, Burnley, Wolves and Sunderland man can be deadly on any day of the week.

WIGAN ATHLETIC
WILL GRIGG

The song 'Will Grigg's on fire' reached the iTunes top 10 last season as the Northern Ireland international fired in 28 goals on top of the 22 he'd struck the season before. Showing no signs that his form had been dampened the 25-year-old began with a bang this term, scoring four times in his first five games. If he's heading for your defence dial 999 in case of emergency.

WOLVES
IVAN CAVALEIRO

As a former goalie, Wolves boss Walter Zenga knows a dangerman when he sees one and broke Wanderers' club record to bring in Portugal international Cavaleiro for a reported £7m. The 23-year-old can play on the wing or up front and has played Champions League football for Benfica and Monaco. As an U21 international he hit a hat-trick on his debut against Switzerland in 2013.

1 Draw back your foot as if you are going to kick the ball

2 Instead of following through, stop your foot over the ball ...

3 ...and push it back behind your other leg while starting to turn your body.

4 Finish turning through 180° and head in the opposite direction.

5 Your unsuspecting opponent will be left standing wondering what just happened!

Johan Cruyff debuted his signature dummy at the 1974 FIFA World Cup. The trick is a brilliant manoeuvre to fool your opponent and change direction.

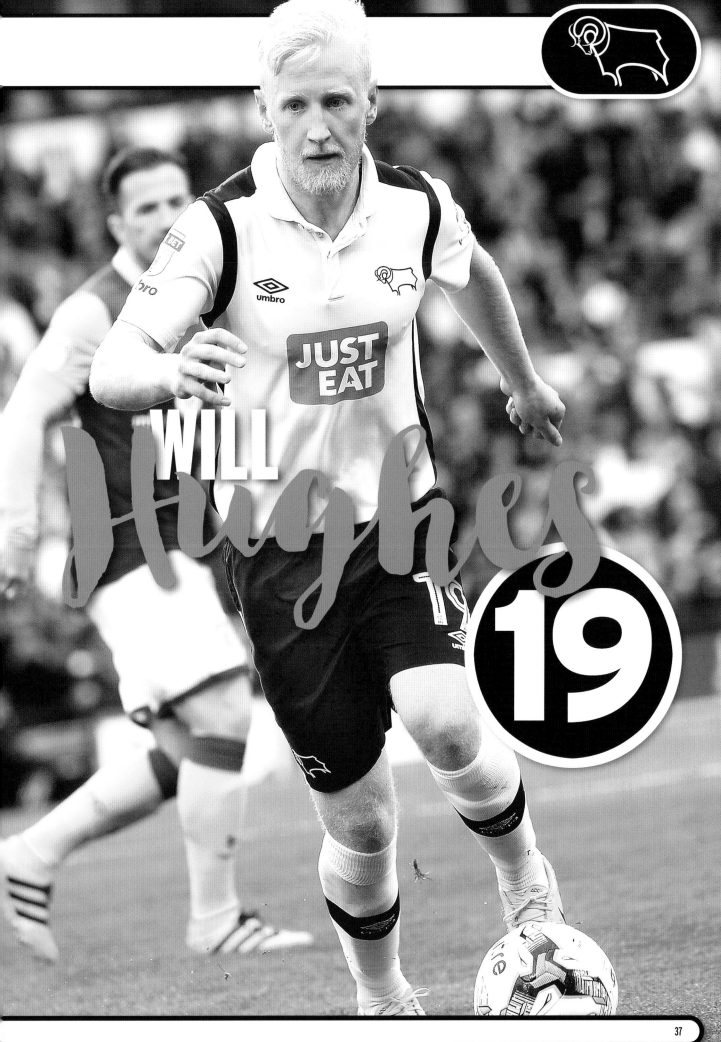

WILL Hughes

19

ARE YER

ROY McFARLAND

A quality footballing centre-half, McFarland went on to manage the Rams after playing 530 times for the club and scoring 49 goals, an incredible total for a defender. Capped 28 times by England and Player of the Year in 1969.

PFA Player of the Year in 1975 as he won his second league title with The Rams, 'Toddy' had been Derby's Player of the Season when the 1971-72 title was won. England international who went on to become a successful manager.

COLIN TODD

PETER SHILTON

Won 34 of his record 125 England caps while a Ram. 'Shilts' played 175 times for Derby, helping the club to fifth place in the top flight in 1989.

DAVID NISH

It's not often a full-back costs a British record transfer fee, but Nish was good enough to get Derby to pay a record £225,000 for his signature in 1972. He didn't disappoint, winning the league and adding to his haul of England caps.

PETER DOHERTY

'Mr. Magic' only played 25 games for Derby, but has to be in any Rams Dream Team. An absolutely brilliant left-winger, he worked in tandem with Raich Carter as Derby won the FA Cup in 1946, Doherty scoring in the final. Played for and managed Northern Ireland.

RON WEBSTER

Twice a title winner in 1971/72 and 1974/75 and Player of the Year in 1973/74. Ron was with Derby from 1960 and played 455 league games before becoming a long-serving youth team coach.

DREAM

RAICH CARTER

ARCHIE GEMMILL

Hard working Scottish international midfielder who captained Derby County to the league title in 1975, his second Championship with the Rams. He was Derby's Player of the Year in 1983/84.

KEVIN HECTOR

Derby's record appearance maker, playing 486 league games. Player of the Year in 1972/73, striker Hector twice won the League at the Baseball Ground and to many is still the 'King.'

TEAM

TED McMINN

Rams Player of the Year in 1991/92, McMinn began with a bang, scoring one of the best goals you could ever see on his home debut against Manchester United in 1988. The 'Tin Man' was an excellent winger on either flank.

STEVE BLOOMER

Steve still sits next to the dug-out 110 years after he finished playing! Bloomer was that good, his bust has pride of place at the stadium. Derby's greatest goalscorer he scored 332 goals for Derby and 28 for England in only 23 games.

The only player to win the cup both before and after World War Two - with derby in 1946 and home town-team Sunderland in 1937. One of England's greatest ever midfielders, he also played cricket for Derbyshire!

DESIGN YOUR OWN
Footie
Boots

CYRUS Christie

2

Here's the second half... A-Z OF THE

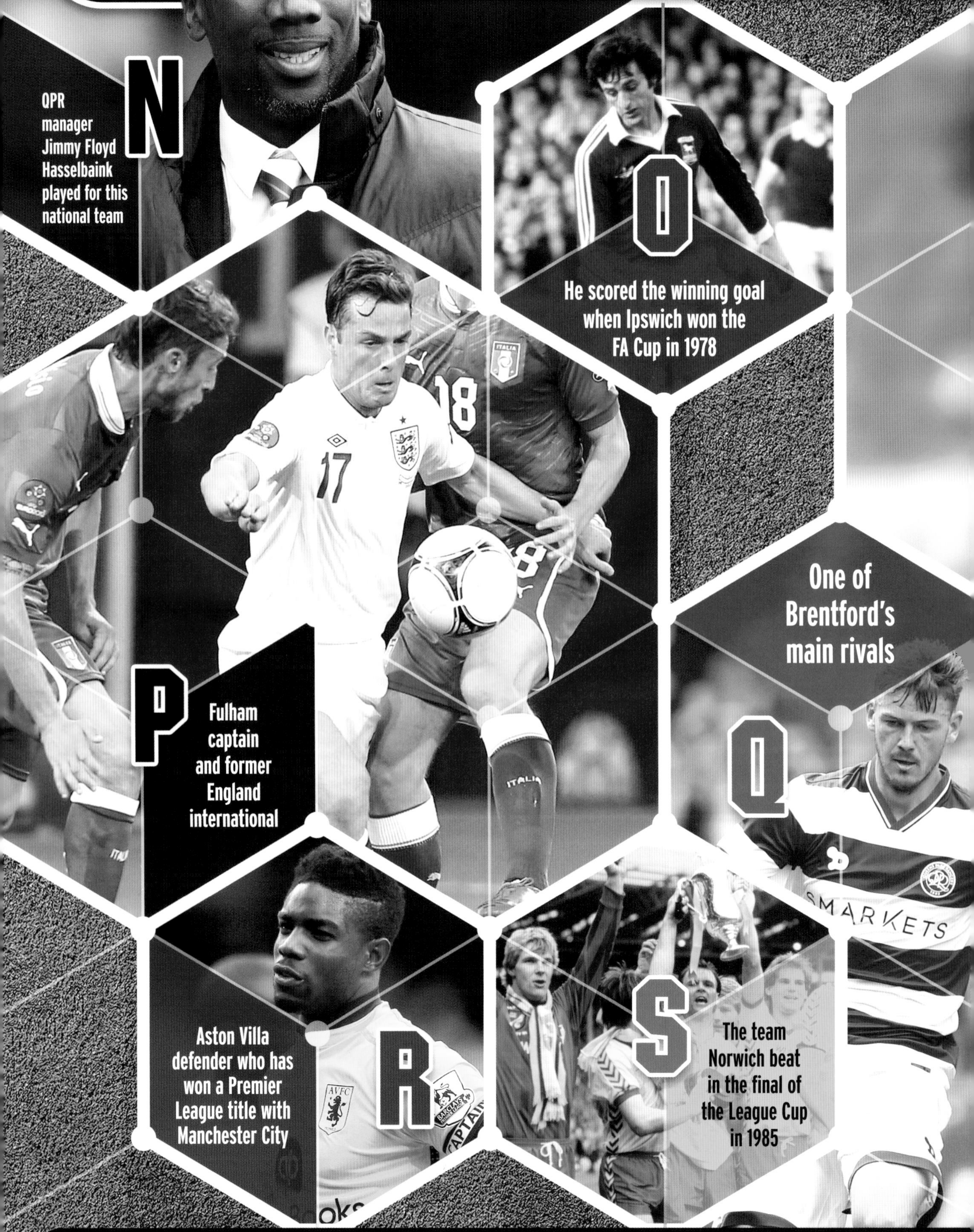

N

QPR manager Jimmy Floyd Hasselbaink played for this national team

O

He scored the winning goal when Ipswich won the FA Cup in 1978

P

Fulham captain and former England international

Q

One of Brentford's main rivals

R

Aston Villa defender who has won a Premier League title with Manchester City

S

The team Norwich beat in the final of the League Cup in 1985

The answer to each clue begins with the corresponding letter of the alphabet

T

U
The animal on Bristol City's crest

W

Barnsley's nickname

Nottingham Forest's number 24

V

Sheffield Wednesday's goalie

X
Newcastle manager, Rafa Benitez, bought and sold this Spanish midfielder while at Liverpool

Y
Young Rotherham forward

Z
Danish striker who signed for Cardiff this summer

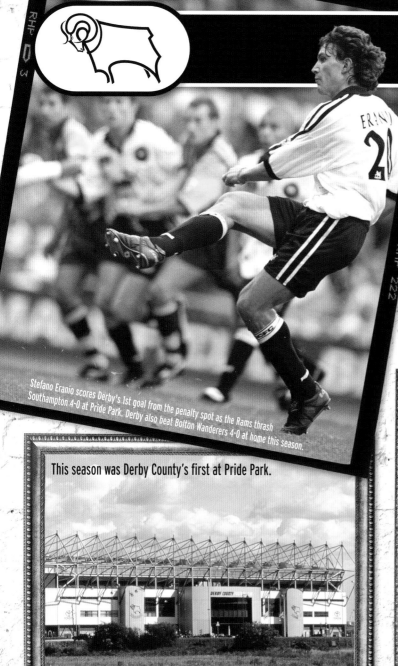

Can you spot the season from these five clues?

Stefano Eranio scores Derby's 1st goal from the penalty spot as the Rams thrash Southampton 4-0 at Pride Park. Derby also beat Bolton Wanderers 4-0 at home this season.

The Rams finished the Premiership campaign in ninth place.

This season was Derby County's first at Pride Park.

Deon Burton arrived from Portsmouth for £1,000,000.

Paulo Wanchope was top of the Rams' scoring charts with 17 goals in all competitions, 13 in the league.

spot the season

TOM

10

Ince

Richard Keogh
REPUBLIC OF IRELAND

RAMS AT THE
Euros

It was a season to remember for Richard Keogh and the summer in France was a fitting way for the Derby County Captain to end his 2015/16 campaign.

After a clean sweep of the end of season awards with the Rams, Keogh was named in Martin O'Neill's 23-man squad.

Although he was named on the bench for the first two of the Green Army's group fixtures, a chance to impress fell Keogh's way against Italy in a game they had to win in order to qualify for the competition's knockout stages.

It was an opportunity that he grasped with both hands and after pulling off a historic 1-0 victory, Keogh kept his place for the knockout game against Euro hosts France, who went on to reach the final of the championships.

...at Euro 2016

Chris Baird
NORTHERN IRELAND

After playing an integral part in Northern Ireland's historic UEFA Euro qualifying campaign, Chris Baird was named in Michael O'Neill's 23-man squad for the tournament in France.

With 77 caps in total for his nation, Baird started in the first of Northern Ireland's group stage games against Poland where they fell to a 1-0 defeat.

Serving as one of the squad's most experienced players, Baird did not feature again in the tournament, however, his influence off the pitch was seen to be just important as the Green and White army made it to the knockout stages of the competition, losing narrowly 1-0 to Wales in the round of 16.

Following the conclusion of the competition, the versatile 34-year-old decided to call time on what had been an illustrious international career.

Cyrus Christie
REPUBLIC OF IRELAND

It was a different sort of experience for Cyrus Christie Euro 2016. Like Richard Keogh, he too was involved in Martin O'Neill's final 23-man squad for the tournament in France and throughout the competition he provided fellow right-back Seamus Coleman with the competition needed to keep him at the top of his game.

In terms of international involvement with his nation, it has been an impressive breakthrough season for Christie in last year.

A model of consistency at club level, Christie was a regular feature during Ireland's UEFA Euro 2016 qualifying campaign making his debut in November 2014 against USA and he scored his first goal for his nation against Gibraltar.

Undoubtedly the experience of being at his first major tournament will be one that he hopes to build on as the Republic of Ireland turn their thoughts to qualifying for the FIFA World Cup in 2018.

IT IS FAIR TO SAY THAT DERBY COUNTY'S
2015/16 CHAMPIONSHIP CAMPAIGN WAS ONE THAT..

Goal
OF THE
SEASON

was full of spectacular goals!

Who can forget George Thorne's outrageous volley away at Huddersfield or Jacob Butterfield's outside-of-the-box screamer against Rotherham United in front of the home fans?

Another goal in particular that stands out for Derby fans everywhere, was when January transfer arrival Marcus Olsson wrote himself into Rams' folklore on that memorable day in March when we beat our Rivals, Forest, from across the A52.

However, out of all the contenders for the Goal of Season Award, it was Bradley Johnson who grabbed the top spot after he finished what was a fine phase of team play against Hull City in the Rams' 4-0 thrashing in April 2016.

In terms of the game itself, it was very much all to play for between the two sides, with Hull looking to keep their hopes of automatic promotion alive and with Derby looking to remain in the promotion race.

It took less than 29 minutes for Derby to get up and running after Johnson netted his first of the game capitalising on a mistake from the Hull defender Curtis Davies.

On 38 minutes, a fantastic phase of team play involving an initial pass from Marcus Olsson and an intelligent one-two pass between Tom Ince and Johnny Russell saw a chance break loose for Bradley Johnson inside the box and he lashed the ball home. It was a fantastic goal and was deservedly awarded the Goal of the Season.

With the match looking set and after the Tigers were reduced to ten men, further salt was rubbed into the wound of the eventual play-off final winners after both Chris Martin and Craig Bryson netted in the dying stages of the game.

23

MATEJ *Vydra*

There are too many footballs in these action shots!
Can you figure out which balls are real!

What ball?

Seven Derby County greats have registered over 500 appearances for the club.

Let's take a brief look at their contribution to the Rams' rich history.

Kevin HECTOR

Record appearance maker Kevin Hector pulled on a Derby County shirt 589 times during two separate spells with the club.

Signed by Tim Ward, Hector joined the club from Bradford Park Avenue in 1966 and proved to be a key player under the management of both Brian Clough and Dave Mackay. He formed a formidable strike partnership with John O'Hare and scored a total of 201 goals for the Rams.

During a wonderful era at the Baseball Ground, Hector helped the side win the Second Division title in 1969 and then go on to twice win the First Division in 1972 and 1975. He was also part of Derby sides that reached the semi-finals of the European Cup, FA Cup and League Cup.

Ron WEBSTER

Born in nearby Belper on 21 June 1943, local boy Ron Webster played his entire Football League career for Derby County and is regarded as being one of the club's most loyal servants.

A tough tackling right-back, Webster became a real fans favourite as he clocked up 535 outings for the Rams between 1960 and 1978.

Part of the highly successful Derby sides under Brian Clough and Peter Taylor, Webster also featured during the equally successful Dave Mackay era. In March 2009, Webster was voted as the best right-back in Derby County history.

Roy MCFARLAND

Another player to enjoy two separate spells at the Baseball Ground, Roy McFarland made 530 appearances for the Rams between 1967 and 1984, before later managing the club in the 1990s.

Signed from Tranmere Rovers in August 1967 by the management team of Brian Clough and Peter Taylor, McFarland starred in the 1968/69 Second Division title-winning side. A classy but committed central defender he won two First Division titles during his Derby career – firstly in 1972 under Clough and secondly in 1975 under Dave Mackay.

A true Derby County legend, he replaced Arthur Cox as Rams' manager in October 1993 and guided the team to the 1993/94 play-off final.

Kevin HECTOR
589

Ron WEBSTER
535

ROY McFARLAND
530

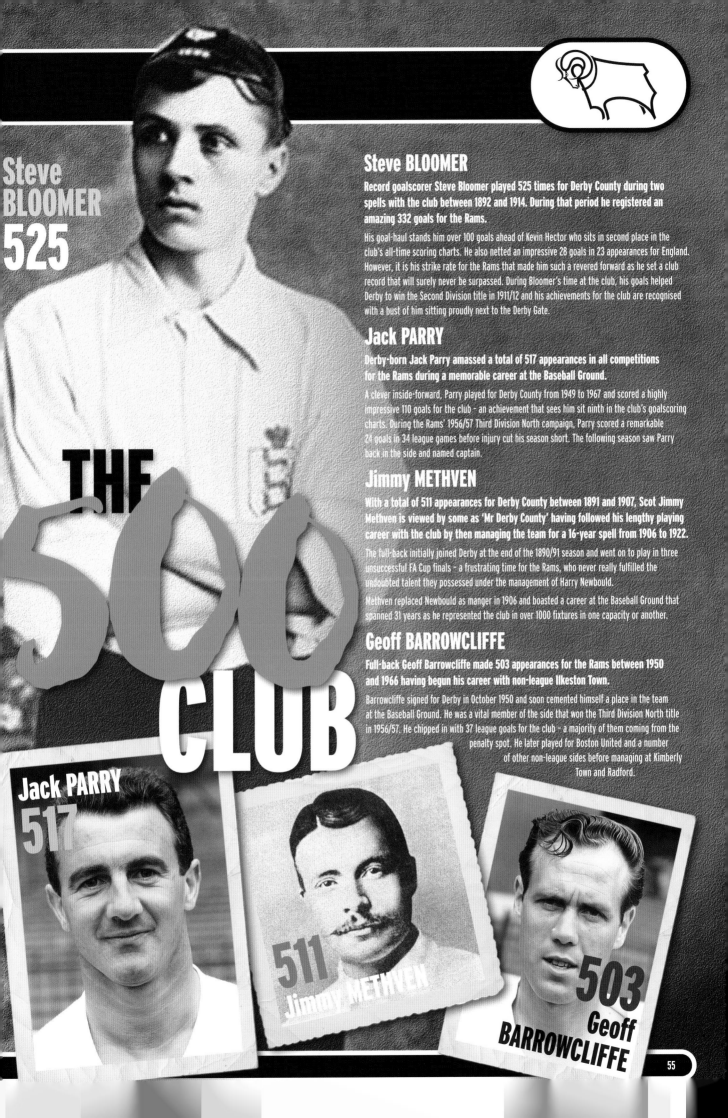

Steve BLOOMER
525

Steve BLOOMER

Record goalscorer Steve Bloomer played 525 times for Derby County during two spells with the club between 1892 and 1914. During that period he registered an amazing 332 goals for the Rams.

His goal-haul stands him over 100 goals ahead of Kevin Hector who sits in second place in the club's all-time scoring charts. He also netted an impressive 28 goals in 23 appearances for England. However, it is his strike rate for the Rams that made him such a revered forward as he set a club record that will surely never be surpassed. During Bloomer's time at the club, his goals helped Derby to win the Second Division title in 1911/12 and his achievements for the club are recognised with a bust of him sitting proudly next to the Derby Gate.

Jack PARRY

Derby-born Jack Parry amassed a total of 517 appearances in all competitions for the Rams during a memorable career at the Baseball Ground.

A clever inside-forward, Parry played for Derby County from 1949 to 1967 and scored a highly impressive 110 goals for the club – an achievement that sees him sit ninth in the club's goalscoring charts. During the Rams' 1956/57 Third Division North campaign, Parry scored a remarkable 24 goals in 34 league games before injury cut his season short. The following season saw Parry back in the side and named captain.

Jimmy METHVEN

With a total of 511 appearances for Derby County between 1891 and 1907, Scot Jimmy Methven is viewed by some as 'Mr Derby County' having followed his lengthy playing career with the club by then managing the team for a 16-year spell from 1906 to 1922.

The full-back initially joined Derby at the end of the 1890/91 season and went on to play in three unsuccessful FA Cup finals – a frustrating time for the Rams, who never really fulfilled the undoubted talent they possessed under the management of Harry Newbould.

Methven replaced Newbould as manger in 1906 and boasted a career at the Baseball Ground that spanned 31 years as he represented the club in over 1000 fixtures in one capacity or another.

Geoff BARROWCLIFFE

Full-back Geoff Barrowcliffe made 503 appearances for the Rams between 1950 and 1966 having begun his career with non-league Ilkeston Town.

Barrowcliffe signed for Derby in October 1950 and soon cemented himself a place in the team at the Baseball Ground. He was a vital member of the side that won the Third Division North title in 1956/57. He chipped in with 37 league goals for the club – a majority of them coming from the penalty spot. He later played for Boston United and a number of other non-league sides before managing at Kimberly Town and Radford.

THE 500 CLUB

Jack PARRY
517

511
Jimmy METHVEN

503
Geoff BARROWCLIFFE

CLUB OR COUNTRY?

1.

2.

3.

4.

5.

6.

7.

8.

9.

spot the Season

Manager Arthur Cox signed Peter Shilton at the end of this season

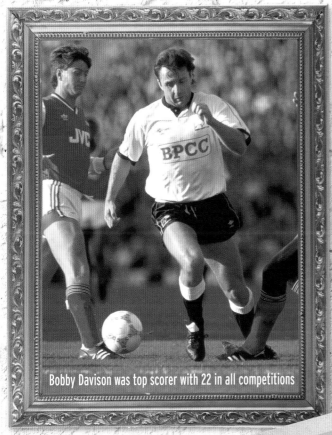

Bobby Davison was top scorer with 22 in all competitions

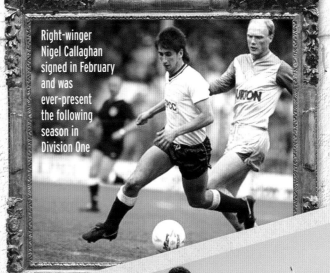

Right-winger Nigel Callaghan signed in February and was ever-present the following season in Division One

Assistant manager Roy McFarland

The Second Division title was won in style, finishing six points ahead of second placed Portsmouth

SKILLS: THE MARADONA SPIN

1
Start off by simply dribbling the ball

2
While moving in a forward motion, tap the ball with your leading foot...

3
...and start turning your body in the opposite direction

4

5
As you're spinning, pull the ball back with your other foot while continuing to turn

6
Then keep moving forward!

Argentinian maestro, Maradona, is very well known for this move. It is brilliant for overcoming opponents and getting yourself into space, as while you are spinning you are putting your back to the defender and shielding the ball.

4

CRAIG

Bryson

PREMIER LEAGUE

PREDICTION FOR PREMIER LEAGUE WINNERS:

Manchester United

YOUR PREDICTION:

PREDICTION FOR PREMIER LEAGUE RUNNERS-UP:

Chelsea

YOUR PREDICTION:

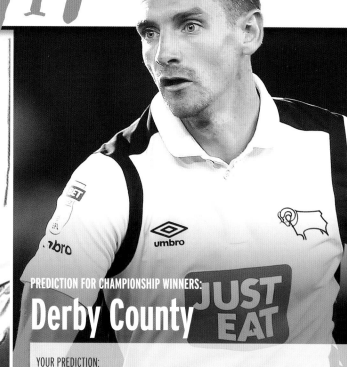

PREDICTION FOR CHAMPIONSHIP WINNERS:

Derby County

YOUR PREDICTION:

PREDICTION FOR ALSO PROMOTED TO THE PREMIER LEAGUE:

Norwich City & Brighton & Hove Albion

YOUR PREDICTION:

THE CHAMPIONSHIP

PREDICTIONS

What do you think will happen in 2017?

THE FA CUP

PREDICTION FOR LEAGUE CUP WINNERS:
Arsenal

YOUR PREDICTION:

PREDICTION FOR LEAGUE CUP FINALISTS:
Manchester City

YOUR PREDICTION:

THE LEAGUE CUP

PREDICTION FOR FA CUP WINNERS:
Liverpool

YOUR PREDICTION:

PREDICTION FOR FA CUP FINALISTS:
Southampton

YOUR PREDICTION:

ANSWERS

PAGE 19: SPOT THE SEASON

1971/72.

PAGE 20: FAN'TASTIC

Nicola Adams, Jessica Ennis-Hill, Andy Murray, Greg Rutherford and Bradley Wiggins.

PAGE 26: A-Z OF THE CHAMPIONSHIP PART ONE

A. Aston Villa. B. Bees. C. Sergi Canos. D. Deepdale.
E. Dave Edwards. F. Falmer Stadium. G. Chris Gunter.
H. Grant Hanley. I. Tom Ince. J. Jussi Jaaskelainen.
K. Kappa. L. Leeds Road. M. Obafemi Martins.

PAGE 31: ON THE ROAD

Aston Villa - Villa Park. Barnsley - Oakwell Stadium. Birmingham - St Andrew's. Blackburn - Ewood Park. Brentford - Griffin Park. Brighton - AMEX Stadium. Bristol City - Ashton Gate. Burton - Pirelli Stadium. Cardiff - Cardiff City Stadium. Derby - iPro Stadium. Fulham - Craven Cottage. Huddersfield - John Smith's Stadium. Ipswich - Portman Road. Leeds - Elland Road. Newcastle - St James Park. Norwich - Carrow Road. Nottm Forest - City Ground. Preston - Deepdale. QPR - Loftus Road. Reading - Madejski Stadium. Rotherham - AESSEAL New York Stadium. Sheff Wed - Hillsborough. Wigan - DW Stadium. Wolves - Molineux Stadium.

PAGE: 38: WHO ARE YER?

A. Craig Bryson. B. Chris Baird. C. Jacob Butterfield.
D. Cyrus Christie. E. Johnny Russell.

PAGE 44: A-Z OF THE CHAMPIONSHIP PART TWO

N. The Netherlands. O. Roger Osborne. P. Scott Parker. Q. QPR.
R. Micah Richards. S. Sunderland. T. the Tykes. U. Unicorn.
V. David Vaughan. W. Keiren Westwood. X. Xabi Alonso.
Y. Jerry Yates. Z. Kenneth Zohore.

PAGE 46: SPOT THE SEASON

1997/98

PAGE 53: WHAT BALL?

Top - D. Bottom - F.

PAGE 57: SPOT THE SEASON

1986/87